Dinosaurs

Brachiosaurus

by Julie Murray

Dash!
LEVELED READERS
An Imprint of Abdo Zoom • abdobooks.com

1

Dash!
LEVELED READERS

Level 1 – Beginning
Short and simple sentences with familiar words or patterns for children who are beginning to understand how letters and sounds go together.

Level 2 – Emerging
Longer words and sentences with more complex language patterns for readers who are practicing common words and letter sounds.

Level 3 – Transitional
More developed language and vocabulary for readers who are becoming more independent.

THIS BOOK CONTAINS
RECYCLED MATERIALS

abdobooks.com

Published by Abdo Zoom, a division of ABDO, PO Box 398166, Minneapolis, Minnesota 55439.
Copyright © 2020 by Abdo Consulting Group, Inc. International copyrights reserved in all countries.
No part of this book may be reproduced in any form without written permission from the publisher.
Dash!™ is a trademark and logo of Abdo Zoom.

Printed in the United States of America, North Mankato, Minnesota.
052019
092019

Photo Credits: Getty Images, Science Source, Shutterstock, ©AStrangerintheAlps p20/CC BY-SA 3.0
Production Contributors: Kenny Abdo, Jennie Forsberg, Grace Hansen, John Hansen
Design Contributors: Dorothy Toth, Neil Klinepier

Library of Congress Control Number: 2018963142

Publisher's Cataloging in Publication Data

Names: Murray, Julie, author.
Title: Brachiosaurus / by Julie Murray.
Description: Minneapolis, Minnesota : Abdo Zoom, 2020 | Series: Dinosaurs |
    Includes online resources and index.
Identifiers: ISBN 9781532127175 (lib. bdg.) | ISBN 9781532128158 (ebook) |
    ISBN 9781532128646 (Read-to-me ebook)
Subjects: LCSH: Brachiosaurus--Juvenile literature. | Dinosaurs--Juvenile
    literature. | Dinosaurs--Behavior--Juvenile literature.
Classification: DDC 567.913--dc23

Table of Contents

Brachiosaurus. 4

More Facts 22

Glossary 23

Index 24

Online Resources 24

Brachiosaurus

Brachiosaurus was a **sauropod** dinosaur. It lived 150 million years ago.

It was very big! It stood 50 feet (15.24 m) tall. It was 80 feet (24.4 m) long.

It may have weighed up to
150,000 pounds (68,038.9 kg).
That is as much as 10 elephants!

It walked on four thick legs. Its front legs were shorter than its hind legs. Its tail helped it **balance**.

It had a very long neck and a small head. Its neck was 25 feet (7.6 m) long!

It could reach the tops of trees for food. It was a plant eater.

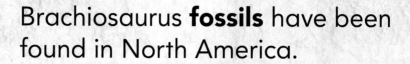

Brachiosaurus **fossils** have been found in North America.

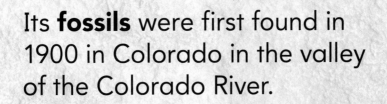

Its **fossils** were first found in 1900 in Colorado in the valley of the Colorado River.

A **replica** of the **fossils** were put together to show the size of the massive dinosaur!

More Facts

- Scientists once thought the brachiosaurus spent time in water. However, today they know the dinosaur lived only on land.

- It traveled in a herd. The herd was made up of about 20 dinosaurs.

- It could eat up to 880 pounds (399 kg) of food each day!

Glossary

balance – to hold steady.

fossil – the remains or trace of a living animal or plant from a long time ago. Fossils are found embedded in earth or rock.

replica – a duplication or copy.

sauropod – a massive, plant-eating dinosaur that had a very long neck, long tail, four legs, and a small head.

Index

Colorado 18

food 14

fossils 17, 18, 20

head 13

legs 10

neck 13

North America 17

size 7, 20

tail 10

weight 8

Online Resources

Booklinks
NONFICTION NETWORK
FREE! ONLINE NONFICTION RESOURCES

To learn more about the Brachiosaurus, please visit **abdobooklinks.com** or scan this QR code. These links are routinely monitored and updated to provide the most current information available.